A Little Muffin Cookbook

Steven Stellingwerf

ILLUSTRATED BY GAIL ROTH

Appletree Press

First published in 1992 by
The Appletree Press Ltd,
19-21 Alfred Street, Belfast BT2 8DL.
Tel. +44 232 243074 Fax. +44 232 246756
Copyright © 1992 The Appletree Press Ltd.
Printed in the E.U. All rights reserved.
No part of this publication may be reproduced
or transmitted in any form or by means, electronic
or mechanical, photocopying, recording or any information
and retrieval system, without permission in writing
from the publisher.

A Little Muffin Cookbook

A catalogue record for this book is
available from the British Library.

ISBN 0-86281-330-1

9 8 7 6 5 4 3 2 1

Introduction

I hope this little book of muffin recipes will show you just how simple muffins are to prepare. Indeed, muffin recipes do not require fancy ingredients or complex preparation to make the result taste good.

Tradition has it that muffins were first baked as a breakfast bread and they are still considered a breakfast pastry worldwide. Through the years, the tradition has changed slightly and muffins are now being considered able to be served at any time of the day, breakfast being the most popular, then lunch and afternoon tea, and even those special holiday feasts with family.

This book is divided into the four seasons of the year, with suggestions for muffins on each of the holidays of those seasons and relying on the availability of seasonal fruit.

A note on measures

Metric, imperial and volume measurements are given for all recipes. For best results use one set only. Spoon measurements are level except where otherwise stated.

Christmas Muffins

The rich, candied fruit-and-sherry taste of these muffins will please hungry appetites on any cold winter morning. They can be served cold or warm and will complement any Christmas brunch table.

1/4 pt/150ml/1/2 cup sherry
3oz/75g/1/3 cup raisins
2oz/50g/1/4 cup candied pineapple, finely chopped
2oz/50g/1/4 cup candied cherries
2oz/50g/1/4 cup slivered almonds
8oz 250g/2 cups flour
2 tsp baking powder
1 tsp salt
1/2 tsp allspice
1/2 tsp ground cinnamon
4oz/100g/1/2 cup sugar
1 egg
3oz/75g/1/3 cup butter, melted
1/2 pt/250ml/1 cup milk
(makes 12)

Pre-heat oven to gas mark 4/350°F/180°C. Soak fruits in sherry overnight in a covered container. In a medium bowl combine flour, baking powder, salt, allspice, cinnamon and sugar until well blended. Add egg, butter, and milk. Stir together until well blended. Fold in fruits and nuts until just mixed. Bake for 20 minutes.

Apple Streusel Muffins

This recipe was shared with me by a very good friend who has been in the catering business for several years. It is one of her most requested muffins.

8oz/225g/2 cups plain flour
8oz/225g/1 cup sugar
1 tbsp baking powder
1 1/4 tsp cinnamon
1 large apple, finely chopped
1/2 tsp baking soda
2 eggs
1/2 pt/250ml/1 cup soured cream
2oz/50g/1/4 cup butter, melted
1/4 tsp salt
Streusel Topping
2oz/100g/1/4 cup sugar
3 tbsp flour
1/2 tsp cinnamon
2 tbsp butter, melted
(makes 18 muffins)

Pre-heat oven to gas mark 4/350°F/180°C. In a large bowl stir together flour, sugar, baking powder, cinnamon, salt and baking soda. Set aside. In a small bowl, beat eggs, soured cream and butter. Add all at once to dry ingredients. Fold in apples, stirring only until slightly blended. Fill muffin tins 2/3 full and sprinkle topping on. Bake for 25–30 minutes.

Hot Cross Muffins

A tasty substitute to serve your guests on Easter morning instead of the regular traditional hot cross buns. Also considered a sweet bread, these muffins blend in well with any Easter meal, whether it be a sunrise brunch or the traditional dinner feast.

8oz/225g/2 cups plain flour
1 tbsp baking powder
$^1/_2$ tsp salt
2 tsp cinnamon
$^1/_2$ tsp nutmeg
4oz/100g/$^1/_2$ cup sugar
1 egg
3oz/80g/$^1/_3$ cup butter, melted
$^1/_2$ pt/250ml/1 cup milk
8oz/250g/1 cup mixed candied fruit, chopped

Icing

8oz/250g/1 cup icing sugar
2 tbsp milk
$^1/_2$oz/15g/1 tbsp melted butter
$^1/_2$ tsp vanilla essence
(makes 12)

Pre-heat oven to gas mark 4/350°F/180°C. Sift flour, baking powder, salt, cinnamon, nutmeg and sugar together. Mix egg, butter and milk into flour mixture until slightly blended. Fold in candied fruits until mixed. Bake for approximately 20 minutes, or until lightly browned. Cool. Beat icing sugar, milk, butter and vanilla essence until well blended, about 3–5 minutes. Pipe a cross on the top of each muffin.

Gingerbread Muffins

Gingerbread Muffins are at their best when served cool. This gives the many spices in the recipe time to reach their full flavour.

2oz/50g/^{1}/4 cup butter at room temperature
6oz/150g/^{2}/3 cup sugar
^{1}/4 cup molasses
I egg
10oz/300g/1 ^{1}/3 cups plain flour
^{1}/2 tsp salt
^{1}/2 tsp baking powder
^{1}/2 tsp soda
2 tsp cinnamon
I tsp ground ginger
^{1}/2 tsp ground cloves
^{1}/2 cup hot water
8oz/200g/I cup raisins
(makes 20-24)

Pre-heat oven to gas mark 4/350°F/180°C. Blend butter and sugar until light and fluffy. Beat in molasses and egg. Add dry ingredients to cream mixture alternately with hot water until well blended. Fold in raisins. Bake for approximately 15 minutes until muffins are golden brown.

Refreshing Lemon Muffins

These muffins are bursting at the seams with the refreshing flavour of lemon and make a light snack when served with afternoon tea. They also complement a bowl of fresh fruit nicely.

8oz/225g/2 cups plain flour
1 tbsp baking powder
1 tsp salt
4oz/200g/1/2 cup sugar
1 egg
1/2 pt/250ml/1 cup milk
5oz/125g/1/3 cup butter, melted
2 tbsp lemon peel, grated
2 tsp lemon essence
1/2 cup pecans, chopped
(makes 18)

Pre-heat oven to gas mark 4/350°F/180°C. Sieve together flour, baking powder, salt and sugar in a small mixing bowl. Add egg, milk and butter stirring until well blended. Fold in lemon peel, lemon extract and pecans so that the batter is slightly mixed. Bake for 20–25 minutes.

Orange Poppy Seed Muffins

Normally served by themselves, Orange Poppy Seed Muffins are easily adapted. They taste wonderful when sliced in half, spread with butter and filled with thinly-sliced ham.

8oz/200g/1 cup sugar
5oz/125g/¹/₃ cup butter at room temperature
1 egg
1 tbsp poppy seeds
¹/₂ tsp soda
2 tbsp orange peel, grated
2 tbsp orange juice
¹/₄ pt/100ml/¹/₂ cup soured cream
5oz/140g/1¹/₃ cups plain flour
¹/₂ tsp salt
(makes 12)

Pre-heat oven to gas mark 4/350°F/180°C. Mix the sugar, soured cream, butter and egg thoroughly. Stir in poppy seeds, baking soda, orange peel, orange juice, flour and salt until slightly blended. Bake for 15–20 minutes or until lightly browned.

Morning Glory Muffins

With its various ingredients and moist texture, this muffin has grown to be one of the most popular baked today. It is so popular, indeed, that some say the Blueberry Muffin has taken second place now to the Morning Glory Muffin.

8oz/225g/2 cups plain flour
10oz/300g/1¼ cups white sugar
2 tsp baking soda
2 tsp cinnamon
½ tsp salt
2 large carrots, grated
4oz/100g/½ cup raisins
4oz/100g/½ cup walnuts, chopped
4oz/100g/½ cup dessicated coconut
½ large apple, grated
3 eggs
½ pt/250ml/1 cup vegetable cooking oil
3 tsp vanilla essence
(makes 24)

Pre-heat oven to gas mark 4/350°F/180°C. In a large bowl combine flour, sugar, soda, cinnamon and salt. Stir in carrots, raisins, nuts, coconut and apple. In a bowl, beat eggs, oil and vanilla essence until well blended. Stir into flour mixture until batter is just slightly combined. Bake for 20 minutes. Do not overbake.

Honey Bran Muffins

So moist, delicious and full of flavour are these muffins that you would never know they are a healthy way to start off the morning.

8oz/200g/1 cup crushed pineapple
12oz/350g/1½ cups wheat-bran cereal
½ pt/150ml/⅔ cup buttermilk
1 egg
2oz/50g/⅓ cup pecans, chopped
3 tbsp vegetable oil
¼ pt/75ml/⅓ cup honey
3oz/85g/⅔ cup whole-wheat flour
½ tsp baking soda
½ tsp salt
(makes 12)

Pre-heat oven to gas mark 4/350°F/180°C. In a large mixing bowl combine undrained pineapple, bran cereal and buttermilk. Let this stand until cereal has soaked up the liquid. Stir in eggs, nuts, oil and ⅓ cup of the honey. In a small bowl mix flour, soda and salt. Stir into bran mixture until slightly blended. Bake for approximately 15–20 minutes until golden brown.

Ginger Pear Muffins

With their spicy flavour and moist texture, these muffins are bound to be a success. Not only can they be eaten with a main meal but, sliced in half with a scoop of ice cream in the centre, they create a wonderfully refreshing dessert.

8oz/225g/2 cups plain flour
6oz/175g/³⁄₄ cup brown sugar, firmly packed
1 tsp baking soda
1 tsp salt
2 tsp ground ginger
1 tsp ground cinnamon
¹⁄₂ tsp ground cloves
¹⁄₂ pt/250ml/1 cup plain yoghurt
¹⁄₄ pt/120ml/¹⁄₂ cup vegetable cooking oil
4 tbsp molasses
1 egg
2 large pears, diced
2oz/50g/¹⁄₃ cup chopped walnuts
(makes 18)

Pre-heat oven to gas mark 4/350°F/180°C. In a large bowl mix flour, brown sugar, baking soda, salt, ginger, cinnamon and cloves until thoroughly mixed. In a separate bowl, blend yoghurt, oil, molasses and egg until well blended. Combine yoghurt mixture to flour mixture until slightly blended. Fold in pears and walnuts. Bake for 25 minutes.

Blueberry Muffins

I can remember being served a warm blueberry muffin with a hot bowl of chilli on cold weather days by my mother. I also remember the story of how her mother served the same meal to her when she was little. Now grown, I still enjoy these muffins with any meal.

12oz/350g/3 cups plain flour
1 tbsp baking powder
$^1/_2$ tsp baking soda
6oz/175g/$^3/_4$ cup sugar
1 $^1/_2$ tsp salt
1 lb/500g/2 cups blueberries
2 eggs
$^3/_4$ cup milk
4oz/100g/$^1/_2$ cup butter, melted
1 tbsp orange peel, grated
$^1/_4$ pt/100ml/$^1/_2$ cup orange juice
1 $^1/_2$ tbsp lemon juice
(makes 24)

Pre-heat oven to gas mark 6/400°F/200°C. Sieve flour, baking powder, baking soda, sugar and salt into a bowl. Add blueberries and roll until coated with flour. In a large mixing bowl, mix eggs, milk, butter, orange peel, orange juice and lemon juice. Add the flour and blueberry mixture and stir until blended. Bake for 20 minutes.

Courgette Muffins

A few years ago my grandmother shared this recipe with me. She considered it to be very good and after trying it, I agree with her that it is a very moist and tasty muffin. It is sure to remain a favourite with successive generations.

---

3 eggs
3 tsp vanilla essence
3 tsp ground cinnamon
1/2 tsp ground nutmeg
12oz/350g/3 cups flour
1/2 pt/250ml/1 cup vegetable oil
2 courgettes, grated
1 lb/500g/2 cups sugar
1 tsp baking soda
1 tsp salt
1 tsp baking powder
(makes 24)

Pre-heat oven to gas mark 4/350°F/180°C. Mix together eggs and vanilla essence, beat until well blended. Add cinnamon, nutmeg, flour, oil and courgette to egg mixture and blend well. Continue to add sugar, baking soda, salt and baking powder and mix until well blended. Bake for 15–20 minutes.

Cranberry Muffins

With its sweet flavour and tart aftertaste this muffin makes a wonderful afternoon-tea sandwich when sliced in half and filled with thinly-sliced turkey. The muffins can be baked in a large muffin tin for regular-size sandwiches, or in a mini-muffin tin for tea sandwiches.

6oz/170g/1 1/2 cups plain flour
4oz/100g/1/2 cup sugar
1 tsp baking powder
1/2 tsp baking soda
1/2 tsp salt
2 eggs
2oz/50g/1/4 cup butter, melted
1/4 pt/100ml/1/2 cup soured cream
1 tsp almond essence
8oz/200g/1 cup fresh or frozen cranberries
(makes 8-12)

Pre-heat oven to gas mark 4/350°F/180°C. Mix together flour, sugar, baking powder, baking soda and salt in a large bowl. In another bowl blend eggs, butter, soured cream and almond essence. Pour egg mixture over flour mixture and blend slightly until just blended. Fold in cranberries until just mixed. Bake muffins for approximately 25–30 minutes.

Peanut Butter Muffins

This is a favourite among children because of its outstanding peanut-butter flavour. Sliced in half and spread with jam, this muffin tastes like a peanut-butter-and-jam sandwich.

4oz/120g/1 cup bran cereal flakes, crushed
6oz/170g/1 1/2 cups plain flour
1 tsp salt
3/4 pt/250ml/1 1/2 cups milk
2oz/50g/4 tbsp butter, melted
5 tbsp brown sugar
3 tsp baking powder
2 eggs
6oz/150g/2/3 cup crunchy peanut butter
(makes 18)

Pre-heat oven to gas mark 4/400°F/200°C. In a bowl mix together the bran, flour, salt, brown sugar and baking powder. In another bowl mix the peanut butter and milk until smooth. Add the eggs and melted butter. Beat well. Combine this with the dry ingredients. Bake for 15–20 minutes or until golden brown.

Banana Muffins

This recipe goes back several generations as a banana loaf bread, passed on to me by my grandmother. To this day she still uses this recipe on special occasions. The unique ingredient is the maraschino cherries which enhance the rich flavour of the bread. I choose to adapt it by baking the recipe in muffin tins instead of loaf tins, which work perfectly.

8oz/200g/1 cup sugar
4oz/100g/^{1}/$_2$ cup butter
2 eggs
1 large mashed ripe banana
8oz/225g/2 cups plain flour
1 tsp baking soda
^{1}/$_2$ tsp salt
4oz/100g/^{1}/$_2$ cup pecans, chopped
4oz/100g/^{1}/$_2$ cups maraschino cherries, chopped
(makes 12)

Pre-heat oven to gas mark 4/350°F/180°C. In a bowl cream sugar, butter and eggs until light and fluffy. Add bananas and beat until well mixed. Add flour, baking soda, salt, pecans and maraschino cherries and mix once again until well blended. Bake for approximately 20 minutes or until golden brown.

Surprise Jam Muffins

Just as this recipe suggests, everyone who samples these muffins will get a surprise. The centre can be filled with all sorts of different jams and jellies depending on the baker's preference.

7oz/200g/1¾ cups plain flour
2oz/50g/¼ cup sugar
2½ tsp baking powder
¾ tsp salt
1 egg
scant ½ pt/200ml/¾ cup milk
⅓ pt/100ml/⅓ cup cooking oil
jelly or jam
(makes 18)

Pre-heat oven to gas mark 4/400°F/200°C. Mix flour, sugar, baking powder and salt. Beat the egg and add milk and oil to the beaten egg. Pour milk mixture over flour mixture. Stir until all the flour is wet and well blended. Fill greased muffin tins ⅓ full. Add 1 teaspoon of jam and then fill each tin with more batter so that it is ⅔ full. Bake for 20 minutes.

Chocolate Chip Muffins

Any chocoholic is bound to love this muffin and its many chocolate chips. Whether you are a chocolate fan or not, you will soon taste how wonderful chocolate can be when baked in a muffin.

8oz/225g/2 cups plain flour
1 tbsp baking powder
1 tsp salt
4oz/100g/¹/₂ cup sugar
6oz/175g/¹/₃ cup brown sugar
1 egg
4oz/100g/¹/₂ cup butter, melted
¹/₄ pt/100ml/¹/₂ cup milk
¹/₄ pt/100ml/¹/₂ cup soured cream
14oz/450g/1³/₄ cups chocolate chips
8oz/200g/1 cup walnuts, chopped
(makes 12)

Pre-heat oven to gas mark 4/350°F/180°C. In a medium bowl combine flour, baking powder, salt and sugars. In another bowl blend egg, butter, milk and soured cream until well blended. Add flour mixture to butter mixture and mix well. Fold in chocolate chips and walnuts. Bake muffins for approximately 15–20 minutes.

Date Muffins

Dates, the main ingredient, are readily available all year round so this is not a seasonal muffin: it's appropriate for any time of the year. These muffins freeze well.

$^1/_2$oz/15g/1 tbsp butter
1 tsp baking soda
$^1/_2$ pt/250ml/1 cup boiling water
8oz/200g/1 cup chopped dates
4oz/100g/$^1/_2$ cup chopped pecans
8oz/200g/1 cup sugar
1 egg yolk
6oz/170g/1$^3/_4$ cups plain flour
1 tbsp vanilla essence
1 tsp salt
(makes 18)

Pre-heat oven to gas mark 4/325°F/160°C. Put butter and baking soda in a small bowl. Add the cup of boiling water to butter and soda. Place dates and nuts in a small bowl and pour boiling-water mixture over them. Cool for approximately 30 minutes. Mix in sugar, egg yolk, flour, vanilla essence and salt. Bake for approximately 20–25 minutes.

Orange Date Muffins

By combining two of the best flavours available, you'll create a muffin that's hard to resist.

8oz/225g/2 cups plain flour
1 tbsp baking powder
1 tsp salt
6oz/150g/³/4 cup sugar
1 egg
4oz/100g/¹/2 cup butter
¹/2 pt/250ml/1 cup milk
peel from 1 orange, grated
¹/3 pt/200ml/¹/3 cup orange juice
8oz/200g/1 cup dates, chopped
8oz/200g/1 cup walnuts, chopped
(makes 12)

Pre-heat oven to gas mark 4/350°F/180°C. Combine flour, baking powder, salt and sugar in a small bowl. In another bowl slightly blend egg, butter and milk. Add flour mixture to this, blending until just mixed. Fold in orange peel, orange juice, dates and walnuts. Bake for approximately 20 minutes.

Strawberry Muffins

When your greengrocers are full of ripe red strawberries, you'll want to try this recipe. Fresh strawberries are the key to the moist flavour of these muffins.

6oz/150g/1½ cups 100% bran cereal flakes
¾pt/450ml/1½ cups milk
2oz/50g/½ cup whole-wheat flour
1 tbsp baking powder
1 tsp salt
6oz/150g/¾ cup brown sugar, firmly packed
1 egg
3oz/75g/⅓ cup butter, melted
12oz/300g/1½ cups finely-chopped fresh strawberries
(makes 12)

Pre-heat oven to gas mark 4/350°F/180°C. Pour milk over bran flakes and let soak for 20 minutes. Sift together flour, baking powder, salt and brown sugar. Add to bran-flakes mixture. Blend well. Stir in egg and butter to flour mixture until just blended. Gently fold in finely-chopped strawberries. Bake for approximately 20 minutes.

Pumpkin Muffins

When the leaves turn autumn colours, when there is a chill in the air, and Hallowe'en is just around the corner, that's the perfect time to try these pumpkin muffins.

---

1 1/2 lb/750g/3 cups sugar
1/2 pt/250ml/1 cup cooking oil
4 eggs
1 1/2 tsp salt
1 tsp cinnamon
2/3 cup water
1 lb/500g/2 cups cooked pumpkin
14oz/400g/3 1/2 cups plain flour
1/2 tsp ground ginger
1/2 tsp ground cloves
2 tsp baking soda
1 1/2 tsp vanilla essence
1 lb/500g/2 cups chopped walnuts
(makes 30)

Pre-heat oven to gas mark 4/350°F/180°C. In a large mixing bowl combine sugar, oil, eggs, salt, cinnamon, water and pumpkin until well blended. Add remaining ingredients and blend well so that batter is mixed thoroughly. Bake for 15–20 minutes.

Cherry Nut Muffins

This is a simple recipe to prepare and bake and proves that muffins do not have to be difficult to prepare to taste good.

8oz/225g/2 cups plain flour
1 tsp baking powder
1 tsp salt
8oz/200g/1 cup sugar
1 egg
3oz/75g/¹/₃ cup butter
¹/₂ pt/250ml/1 cup milk
8oz/200g/1 cup pecans, chopped
8oz/200g/1 cup maraschino cherries, chopped
(makes 18)

Pre-heat oven to gas mark 4/350°F/180°C. In a medium bowl combine flour, baking powder, salt and sugar. Mix until well blended. Add egg, butter and milk and stir until just mixed together. Fold in pecans and cherries. Bake for approximately 20 minutes.

Rhubarb Muffins

This is considered a summer muffin, since rhubarb is always plentiful during the summer season. Rhubarb, however, can be chopped and frozen ahead of time, to be used all year round.

10oz/250g/1¼ cups brown sugar, firmly packed
1 egg
¼ pt/125ml/½ cup oil
2 tsp vanilla essence
½ pt/250ml/1 cup buttermilk
12oz/300g/1½ cups diced rhubarb
12oz/350g/2½ cups plain flour
1 tsp baking soda
1 tsp baking powder
½ tsp salt
Topping
½oz/15g/1 tbsp butter, melted
3oz/75g/⅓ cup sugar
2 tsp cinnamon
(makes 20)

Pre-heat oven to gas mark 6/400°F/200°C. In a bowl, combine the brown sugar, egg, oil, vanilla essence and buttermilk, mixing until well blended. Add the rhubarb and mix until folded in. In a separate bowl, stir together the flour, soda, baking powder and salt. Add the dry ingredients to the rhubarb batter. Stir until just blended. Sprinkle each muffin with the butter, sugar and cinnamon topping. Bake for 20–25 minutes.

Maple Muffins

As maple syrup was first developed in the southern United States, these have always been considered to be traditional southern muffins. Through the years they have worked their way north via friends and relatives and are now enjoyed throughout America.

8oz/225g/2 cups plain flour
1 tbsp baking powder
1/2 tsp salt
2oz/50g/1/4 cup sugar
1 egg
1/2 pt/250ml/1 cup milk
4oz/100g/1/2 cup butter
2/3 pt/200ml/2/3 cup maple syrup
2 tsp maple essence
8oz/200g/1 cup walnuts, chopped
(makes 12-18)

Pre-heat oven to gas mark 4/350°F/180°C. In a small bowl mix flour, baking powder, salt and sugar. Add egg, milk, butter, maple syrup and maple essence and blend until well mixed. Fold in walnuts until slightly blended. Bake for approximately 20–25 minutes.

Pineapple
Oatmeal Muffins

Pineapple Oatmeal Muffins

These two unique ingredients complement each other so well that you will be amazed at how moist and delicious these muffins are. I know this recipe will be considered one of your favourites.

$^1/_4$ pt/100ml/$^1/_2$ cup vegetable oil
$^1/_8$ pt/50ml/$^1/_4$ cup orange juice
2 eggs
4oz/100g/$^1/_2$ cup brown sugar, firmly packed
2 tsp grated orange rind
12oz/300g/1$^1/_2$ cups rolled oats
8oz/200g/1 cup crushed pineapple, with juice
6oz/175g/1$^1/_2$ cups plain flour
1 tbsp baking powder
1 tsp baking soda
1 tsp salt
(makes 18)

Pre-heat oven to gas mark 4/350°F/180°C. In a large mixing bowl combine oil, orange juice, eggs, brown sugar and orange rind. Mix until well blended. Fold in oats and pineapple. Add flour, baking powder, baking soda and salt. Mix together and blend well. Bake for 20–25 minutes.

Raspberry Muffins

These muffins have always been one of my favourites. The taste of raspberries is so refreshing that I can never resist having a second one.

8oz/225g/2 cups plain flour
1 tsp salt
1 tbsp baking powder
6oz/150g/²⁄₃ cup sugar
1 egg
¹⁄₂ pt/100ml/¹⁄₂ cup milk
1 tsp vanilla essence
3oz/75g/¹⁄₃ cup butter, melted
¹⁄₂ pt/100ml/¹⁄₂ cup soured cream
1 lb/500g/2 cups raspberries
(makes 12)

Pre-heat oven to gas mark 4/350°F/180°C. Stir together flour, salt, baking powder and sugar. Blend in egg, butter, milk, soured cream and vanilla essence. Gently fold in raspberries. Bake for 20 minutes.

Peach Muffins

Peach muffins are easy to prepare and are very economical; with the versatility of using tinned peaches instead of seasonal fresh peaches, the cost stays low and the muffins can be made year round.

4oz/100g/¹/₂ cup butter at room temperature
12oz/300g/³/₄ cup sugar
1 egg
6oz/150g/1¹/₂ cups plain flour
2 tsp baking powder
2 tsp vanilla essence
¹/₂ tsp salt
¹/₄ pt/100ml/¹/₂ cup plain yoghurt
8oz/200ml/1 cup chopped tinned peaches,
well drained
8oz/200g/1 cup chopped pecans
(makes 15)

Pre-heat oven to gas mark 4/350°F/180°C. Cream butter and sugar until fluffy. Add egg and beat well. Beat in vanilla essence and yoghurt. Stir in flour, baking powder and salt. Add peaches and pecans until just blended. Bake for 20 minutes or until lightly browned.

Black Cherry Muffins

The distinctive flavour of these muffins makes them a great favourite. They're best when served cooled and spread with butter. Serve them as a refreshing delight with any spring morning brunch.

8oz/225g/2 cups plain flour
I tbsp baking powder
¹/₂ tsp salt
4oz/100g/¹/₂ cup butter at room temperature
6oz/150g/²/₃ cup sugar
2 eggs
2 tsp vanilla essence
¹/₄ pt/100ml/¹/₂ cup milk
12oz/300g/1¹/₂ cups pitted black cherries, chopped
(makes 12)

Pre-heat oven to gas mark 4/350°F/180°C. In a medium bowl mix flour, baking powder and salt. Dust I tablespoon of the flour mixture into the cherries. Cream butter and sugar until light and fluffy. Add egg and vanilla essence and continue to beat for 3 more minutes. Blend in flour mixture alternately with milk. Fold in cherries until just slightly mixed. Bake for 25 minutes.

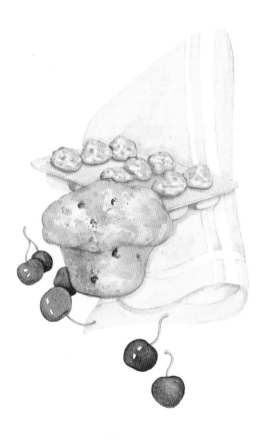

Sweet Potato Muffins

Though similar to the Pumpkin Muffin, the Sweet Potato Muffin has a unique and subdued flavour of its own. This moist muffin is delicious when served as a bread with any main meal. Sweet potatoes, or yams, are available in good greengrocers or West Indian stores.

4oz/100g/½ cup butter
10oz/275g/1¼ cups sugar
2 eggs
10oz/250g/1¼ cups mashed sweet potatoes (yams)
6oz/150g/1½ cups plain flour
2 tsp baking powder
½ tsp salt
1 tsp cinnamon
1 tsp nutmeg
½ pt/250ml/1 cup milk
4oz/100g/½ cup pecans, chopped
4oz/100g/½ cup raisins
(makes 24)

Pre-heat oven to gas mark 4/350°F/180°C. Cream butter and sugar until light and fluffy. Add eggs and mix well. Blend in sweet potatoes. Add dry ingredients and spices alternately with the milk and mix slightly. Fold in pecans and raisins. Bake for 25 minutes.

Index